I0880131

Smog Mother

Also by John Wall Barger

Pain-proof Men
Hummingbird
The Book of Festus
The Mean Game
Resurrection Fail

Chapbooks

The Vnfortunate Report & Tragicall Tidings of Leslie Barger
Samovar/Dukkha
Dying in Dharamsala
The Kindness Machine
Trying on the Walrus Costume in the Ed Sullivan Theater of the Mind

SMOG MOTHER

JOHN WALL BARGER

Copyright © John Wall Barger 2022
All rights reserved

Palimpsest Press
1171 Eastlawn Ave.
Windsor, Ontario. N8S 3J1
www.palimpsestpress.ca

Printed and bound in Canada
Cover design and book typography by Ellie Hastings
Edited by Jim Johnstone

Palimpsest Press would like to thank the Canada Council for the Arts and the Ontario Arts Council for their support of our publishing program. We also acknowledge the assistance of the Government of Ontario through the Ontario Book Publishing Tax Credit.

Canada Council for the Arts | Conseil des Arts du Canada
ONTARIO ARTS COUNCIL
CONSEIL DES ARTS DE L'ONTARIO
an Ontario government agency
un organisme du gouvernement de l'Ontario
ONTARIO CREATES | ONTARIO CRÉATIF

LIBRARY AND ARCHIVES CANADA CATALOGUING IN PUBLICATION

TITLE: Smog mother / John Wall Barger.
NAMES: Barger, John Wall, 1969- author.
IDENTIFIERS: Canadiana (print) 20220278741
Canadiana (ebook) 2022027875X

ISBN 9781990293214 (SOFTCOVER)
ISBN 9781990293221 (EPUB)
ISBN 9781990293238 (PDF)
SUBJECTS: LCGFT: POETRY.
CLASSIFICATION: LCC PS8603.A734 S66 2022 | DDC C811/.6—DC23

for Cal

Table of Contents

Smog Mother / 11

On a Metro at the Edge of the Jungle where Tigers Walked / 25
Fireflies / 26
Bathroom Attendant in Tai Po Megamall / 27
100 Doves Released for Wedding Pictures at Swan Lake in Hefei, Anhui Province, China / 28
An Old Man in Black Slippers at Rush Hour / 29
Woman on a Hong Kong Bus at Night / 30
Dithyramb for a Troubled Man in Yau Ma Tei / 31
Ode to Festival Walk Mall / 32

Samovar / 37

At the Củ Chi Tunnels / 49
A Girl on Khaosan Road Selling Lottery Tickets Gently Hides Her Two Withered Arms / 50
Public Cremation, Pashupatinath Temple, Kathmandu / 51
Naked Woman at a Roadside Buffet / 52
One Given When I'd Ceased to Look / 53

Dying in Dharamsala / 57
By the Halal Chicken Shop / 59
Parking Lot, Tibetan Parliament-in-Exile, Noon / 60
A Stop on the Night Bus / 62
Cryptoscopophilia / 64
Delirious in the Pink House / 65
Beauty Too Close / 67
Dead Calf by the Road / 68
Sipping Tequila with a Friend on My Roof under the Cold Blowtorch Moon / 69

Dukkha / 73

On a North Train to Casarsa, Midwinter, Thinking of *Franny and Zooey* / 85
Bergamo Airport, 3:30 a.m. / 86
Bullfight, Plaza México / 87

Notes / 93
Acknowledgments / 99
About the Author / 101

SHE: The reconstructions have been made as authentically as possible.
The films have been made as authentically as possible.
The illusion, it's quite simple, the illusion is so perfect that tourists cry.
One can always scoff, but what else can a tourist do, really, but cry?

— *Hiroshima Mon Amour,* Marguerite Duras

Smog Mother

The soul is silent.
If it speaks at all
it speaks in dreams.
— Louise Glück

I stand before a large ceramic jug
at the Siriraj Medical Museum,
Bangkok. There'd been a fire
at a cinema, 1970. A boy,
instead of escaping with his family,
climbed into a jug of water.
That made sense. Then
the water grew hot, boiled.
They found him curled up
in the shape of the jug.

I

Thai volunteer protester of faithful bones
You stomp the immense thoroughfare
One hundred thousand souls
The Democracy Monument is wrapped in black
The sharp wings of it are cloaked
O gentle offended ones
Which like clouds have no face
When your heart marches out to die
When you march out to kill
The crowds are crawling waves
I don't know what is next where to be
The further one travels
The less one knows says Lao Tzu
I walk write eat applaud
I weep scrutinize destroy

A military junta has taken the country
The National Council for Peace and Order
Protest leader Sutin Tharatin was shot dead
Tharatin was giving a speech
Now Cambodians are fleeing Thailand
Sutin Tharatin! Sutin Tharatin!
The crowds sing his name
His corpse sprouts stories
One book under another sprouts
From that sudden corpse
The world says this is Thailand's business
Who gives a fuck about them anyway?
Who cares about them
Their whores and cockfights
Anyway?

We clap and clap and clap
We cannot get enough clapping
Loudspeakers bleat slogans
Ideology is rampant in the streets
You can cut doors and windows out of nothing
You can make a room out of nothing
You can slash an idea
You can electrify an idea
You can shove shit into the mouth of an idea
This turns to hate
Better to claw at empty space
Soon there will be nothing
Nothing for all these winds to play on

In the wake of a mighty army
Under so brutal a sun
You must walk unhurried or collapse
O tourist open your wallet of glimmering gold
O tourist at this wat of barbed spires
O tourist you stop to watch the marchers
Your face Christ-haunted frightened
The crowds are singing Sutin Tharatin!

Monks glide among the protesters
Theravāda monks in loose orange robes
Some monks look calm amused even
Among them Khruba Siwichai giggles
Dead seventy-five years but still he giggles
He drifts under a billboard of the king
Beloved King Bhumibol Adulyadej
The king peers down upon us
O frail god face bland unsmiling
Khruba Siwichai giggles
Beware the newly rich
Beware the devourers of corpses

Vagabonds stagger through the crowd
Vagabonds in black rags skin grimy as sadhus
They trudge against the bodies
They wade the human tide
Stomachs hard and hollow as wood
These are household gods
They have never heard tell
Of The National Council for Peace and Order
One is holding a broken machete
One has plastic bags for shoes
He sleeps in a cardboard box beside the ATM
The one in his Spider-Man underwear
He sleeps in the alley beside my guest house

I follow a three-legged dog off the wide boulevard
She hops to a marshaling yard
Emaciated chickens stand in bamboo cages
A family is huddled silent by a fire
The fire a goblin spits spits
The dog wags her scabby tail
She trots into a labyrinth of shanties
Ramshackle shantytown doors walls roofs
Immeasurable corrugated metal
On an unpropitious day in the observation of

Bamboo huts propped on stilts in a muddy river
Wide open is the gate
A parrot-footed boy cries standing in a bucket
I lean to tousle his hair
I cannot help myself
He twists away like a released balloon
O reader listen closely lean in yes you just you yes

The city wails dementedly
The city a dog howling at an ambulance
The city reminds us to praise
Praise the moon! it says
Praise a green leaf! it says
Praise the hem of a robe! it says
The city leans down over me
The city whispers in my ear
I run my hands along its screen door veneer
I hear the yellow song of the scooters
Song of the painted trucks
The painted trucks heaving smoke rings
Every thing that lives heaves out the smog
Smog hangs in the air like a song
We step inside a fog of sleep
It is a cave we are its Minotaurs
We growl against the intrusion
A hero has come uninvited

II

Smog Mother your one broken heel
Smog Mother walking the edges of Bangkok at dusk
Smog Mother at the edges of the property
You chew gum on the edges of praise
You drag eyeliner along the banks of the river
Your fake leather purse is filled with burning bodies
There is defiance in your eyes Smog Mother
You have swallowed Bangkok whole
You are the snake that ingested Bangkok
The 7-Elevens glitter within you
The TVs inside the open doors of the alley glitter
They are lovely fake diamonds
They glitter along your broken heels
The flowering bird the crystal the virgin the dagger

Smog Mother you provide us your milk
We are your children
Weaned on the milk of your praise

Mother Smog I do not like the heroes
The heroes on TV whispering eloquent speeches
Their speeches echo across us
Here is a clear-eyed boy his shirt in shreds
Seated crosslegged on the sidewalk
He tosses pigeons bits of white bread
Beside a field of poppies junk and poppies
Here is a woman on the curb
She hums what might be the *Hawaii Five-O* theme song
Her legs swollen tangled naked
Under wave after wave of passersby
Into the smog de profundis without thee

Mother Smog protector of the people
Mother Smog nobis fiducia save us from evil forever
Direct us by thy grace Smog Mother
The sharp pagodas against the sky your nipples
The toxic streams your feral juices
Such waters of a perennial spring
The dogs are sleepy all day
The dogs are manic and vicious at night
The dogs your breath
At karaoke an old man heard the mountain
The old man your antenna
The teeming markets pregnant with thy glory
Smog Mother with your huge migrant worker's bag
You hobble through alleys
You shot Sutin Tharatin down
The fog of strife your greatest joy
Save us guide us give us wings
Smog Mother drag our sky into the future

III

Beside this river I crouch
I don't know what is next
I present my finger to a bony white cat
The cat will not smell it
Her skin flaps at the dugs
In the dense heat she steps slow
All the cats step slow
The thin haunted hunted cats
Their fur patchy dirty scabby
They lie on the sidewalk like vagabonds
They lie in the path of dogs and scooters
This cat pretends I do not exist
I crouch in her world of no return
Neither of us moves
The sword in my heart blazes
I walk too fast with worry and stress
I'm sorry for things I've done
I'm sorry for things I haven't done
Unpeaceful

Men sit in a circle beside the Chao Phraya River
Fishermen in T-shirts drink beer at a table
The slender water buses glide in glide in
Women hug their grocery bags
Sisters daughters wives grandmothers
The toxic river splashes us all

A boy lies on the tourist path face down palm up
I surprise him
He shivers
One of his eyes on me

Serious as an owl in a tree
He collects himself peels a candy
While I breathe while I breathe
He drops the wrapper in the river
It floats past slow
Slow as a smoke ring on a windless day

A Styrofoam cup floats past
I sit on the bank
Paper plates plastic straws French fries
Lean in can you see it
The body is it a rat yes there

A girl and boy flirt like horses
Gum falls from the boy's mouth
Into beige river water
The girl nabs the gum
Chews it smiles whispers to him
All esses and vees
My love you held me by the river
My love you held me under
My love your bodies filled so many graves
My love how can you be so weary and so young

A bride rises out of a swamp of cars
She is very drunk cursing
Dress hiked up
A wounded swan collapsing
They take her picture with their phones
She is waving waving
Wings of trash
They carry her off in a pong of fried fish

This old man has the biggest ears in the world
The hardened shock in his eyes familiar
What the sun does not touch
One hand folded in the other
He moves calm as a cat
He inches past the market stands
The stands of T-shirts rock like cotton boats
A plastic flower tucked behind his ear
He is filthy
His face emits a minute light

I have a fantasy I die in Bangkok
In a bamboo hut with a street girl
A comical debridement
Goodbye goodbye
Though I have not been with a street girl
I have done worse
Luther told a disciple seeking grace
Sin bravely

An orange-clad monk reads from a cloth book
I think it is scripture
No it is verse
I think it is ribald
His lips stone still his eyes ferocious
I do not blink or ask the way
I do not ask what path we're on
Though I am so far from my guest house!
This foliage this dream unremembered
Praise the lord!
Hallelujah!
I became a full-time worker in His holy vineyard
I became a father to a toxic river

Yeats says all that is personal soon rots
The smiles between these mothers grilling goat
The inborn cravings of this child
Bread in the stomach
A thin grimy dress over beauty
So it must be packed in ice or salt he says

Human history is you Smog Mother
Naked upon a tightrope
Smog Mother your body of yellow light
The world suspended
The world its mountains its fields
Its muggy afternoon wind
My spirit scatters
The wind can find no limbs of mine to play on

I follow a naked man through traffic
He is skinny bent faltering
He is the ugliest human on earth
His forehead a cauliflower
His neck skin a cluster of grapes
His eye stares out of a cave sorrowful
I sit beside him on a curb
He starts to speak

A huge man with greasy lips pulls up on a scooter
He tells me he has a sister
Be good to her I say please brother

Two steps to the left is a glass jar.
An arm inside. A left arm,
chopped. At the elbow,
gristle and veins burst out
like the wires of a radio.
Fog-white, the skin, fog-yellow.
On the forearm a tattoo:
a blue-green man ambles
down the road in formaldehyde fog.
He carries a fish on a string.
He wears a pointed hat.
He smokes a pipe. No,
it's a flute. The way he ambles
he must be a musician.
He is coming from the river.
Has spent all day at the river.
Walks the long way home,
nice and slow, by the poppy field.
He is penniless. He owes
everybody. But tonight
he has dinner. You can sense
his joy in the way he plays
what he learned from the river.
He sings,
            O ferryman, take me home.
I don't have a penny
but I'll play you a song.
When my wife gets a whiff,
even she will forgive me.
When she sees this glittering fish.

On a Metro at the Edge of a Jungle where Tigers Walked

A hardbitten lady holding a tiny radio
in two hands like a hobo with a hat
smiles. The very merest gesture.
A grin like a flag or a noose—
something broken free and scattered
in the four winds. Rain taps
the windows. She gets off but her grin
flutters on, moth in a dark hall.
A memory crawls like a scorpion
out of a shoe: a boxing match on TV
I once sat on a dirt road to watch
with locals in Palawan. Pacquiao,
crowd favorite, hammered De La Hoya.
We cheered. Before the ninth,
De La Hoya's corner threw in the towel.
Handsome De La Hoya, eye mashed
shut, mouth twisted, a punctured
balloon of a man, smashed bust
of a god. Our collective error
and our flaming heart. He grinned.

Fireflies

Who was it that said consciousness
lingers, briefly, after we die?
A florist chain-smokes, stooped
in his outhousey stall.
He breaks each rose stem's neck.
Over his glasses a woman
who is beautiful lights a cigarette.
She buys one white tulip.
He holds it between them,
a kind of candle. Later, she hops away
over a puddle, her cigarette tip
tracing a word in the dark.
The florist wipes his glasses,
as if wondering at the grace
of these embers.
As if his brain were going cold.

Bathroom Attendant in Tai Po Megamall

Urinals are fools, drooling, spitting.
A toilet coughs, backwashing
like a ferry pulling in. The attendant—
resembling a wrinkled schoolkid
in his lime-green tunic, black pants,
black shoes—leans on his red broom,
bracing against an unseen opposition,
peering into the glaucomic blaze
of the pharmacy. His paralytic left hand
he keeps tucked in his pocket,
wiping piss drops with his right.
Men breeze past zipping their flies,
drying fingers like landed gentry.
Some drop coins at his feet.
His father said, of men, there are three kinds:
1. Those who do not finish a job;
2. Those who finish; 3. Those who finish
beautifully. The Great Proletarian
Cultural Revolution did away with
the latter two. So the attendant
leans on his red broom, absorbed by
the Hungry Ghost parade of faces,
girl-dolls lapping ice cream off their fingers;
Manbabies smirking at smartphones.
Nobody watches but he watches
like a kid in a car, head on the window.

100 Doves Released for Wedding Pictures at Swan Lake in Hefei, Anhui Province, China

As the wedding party packs up,
doves circle the park. Local picknickers—
watching doves land, peck grass
—converge on them, a kind of river
jumping its banks, sudden Olympians
leaping flowerbeds toward the birds.
A thin man in suit and tie
slips in the mud. A jogger bites
a living dove. Screams and giggles
fill the air. The idea of time
comes from the Greek, *Hōra*,
a goddess in a leopard-skin
leotard who escaped her frenzied
suitors by hiding in a well
with her pet cricket, Cerberus.
A dove flaps inside a church
of fingers. Boys wade the lake.
A baby girl totters in the grass.
Her grandmother slides a thumb
into a dove, tears it in half,
drops the slick plump breast
into a plastic bag, tosses the rest
beside the girl. The grandfather,
humming, lights the grill.

An Old Man in Black Slippers at Rush Hour

inches uphill, pushing
a trolley heaped with meat.
His eyes furnace flues.
Taking a drag off the cigarette
singeing his knuckles,
he hovers amid shoppers
like a Hiroshige hawk, claws
dangling. A woman with a look
of studied indifference
brushes against him,
winces, flicks her sleeve—
as if after his beheading
she had mistakenly dipped
her handkerchief in his blood.

Woman on a Hong Kong Bus at Night

scowls when I sit next to her.
Before I read two lines of my book
she nods off, leans on my arm,
head on my shoulder. Through my shirt
I feel teeth grinding, lips
forming ghosts of words, a trickle
of drool on my hand. O such things
reach inside a man! Any wetness
on the skin and we long for
the first shores. My wife, who I love,
is in the seat behind me
and the woman shifts and moans
as if unfastening her nudity.
I wish this were a different world—
one where we could lean on a stranger
without shame. This life is torture,
torquere, twisting the child out of the adult.
The bus jolts, she wakes, retreats.
Out the window, glass towers, banks.
On my skin, her warmth.

Dithyramb for a Troubled Man in Yau Ma Tei

An avalanche of Cantonese tumbles
out of him, a fire hydrant gushing
refutations of otherworldly arraignments.
He's radiant, fearless. I'm carried
out of my seat by eddies of admiration.
In his eyes a dog tore free of its leash
and runs down cars and we know
how that ends. Freedom of the heart,
yes, maybe, the kind that drifts downriver
unmoored whirling whirling toward
the next cursed station, while *lo* the shores
recede. I read about a plant in the Sahara,
the Anastatica, a resurrection plant
they call it, that can be dormant
100 years, withering, gray, leafless,
branches curling into a tight ball
till in a certain rainfall at a certain hour
it germinates and bursts (bursts!)
with white flowers. He licks his split lip
and sniffs the air as if remembering.

Ode to Festival Walk Mall

Uterus of silence!
In your food court inner ear
Adderall schoolkids
smeared with McDonald's
ketchup and anxiety
tap out a chaotic reveille
with plastic spoons and cups
upon your deathless
plastic tables. Their song trails them
on hind legs, urinating, a fool.
O great rumbling dam
of plastic! O Pharos, tower
trembling with citizens!
Seer, you foretell an age
of merciless utility, nothing futile.
You demand that this poem—
cobbled from handprints
on Bank of China glass,
scuffs of vigor on the escalator,
grins of tiny figure skaters
—be wiped clean. *Look*,
in a million square feet of buffed tiles,
this one broken bottle
quivers with dusk like a tattoo
on a dead woman's hand
only to be swept away
before my eyes. And *look*,
outside: the banyan tree,
its unruly veins,
its branches straining sunwards.
Is it a musical instrument?

Who would play it?
Cruelty springs within me,
violence I swallow
with a bite of Häagen-Dazs.
An inorganic smell
pervades the cinema:
scornful, desiccated,
prelapsarian. A skeleton
requiring a future.

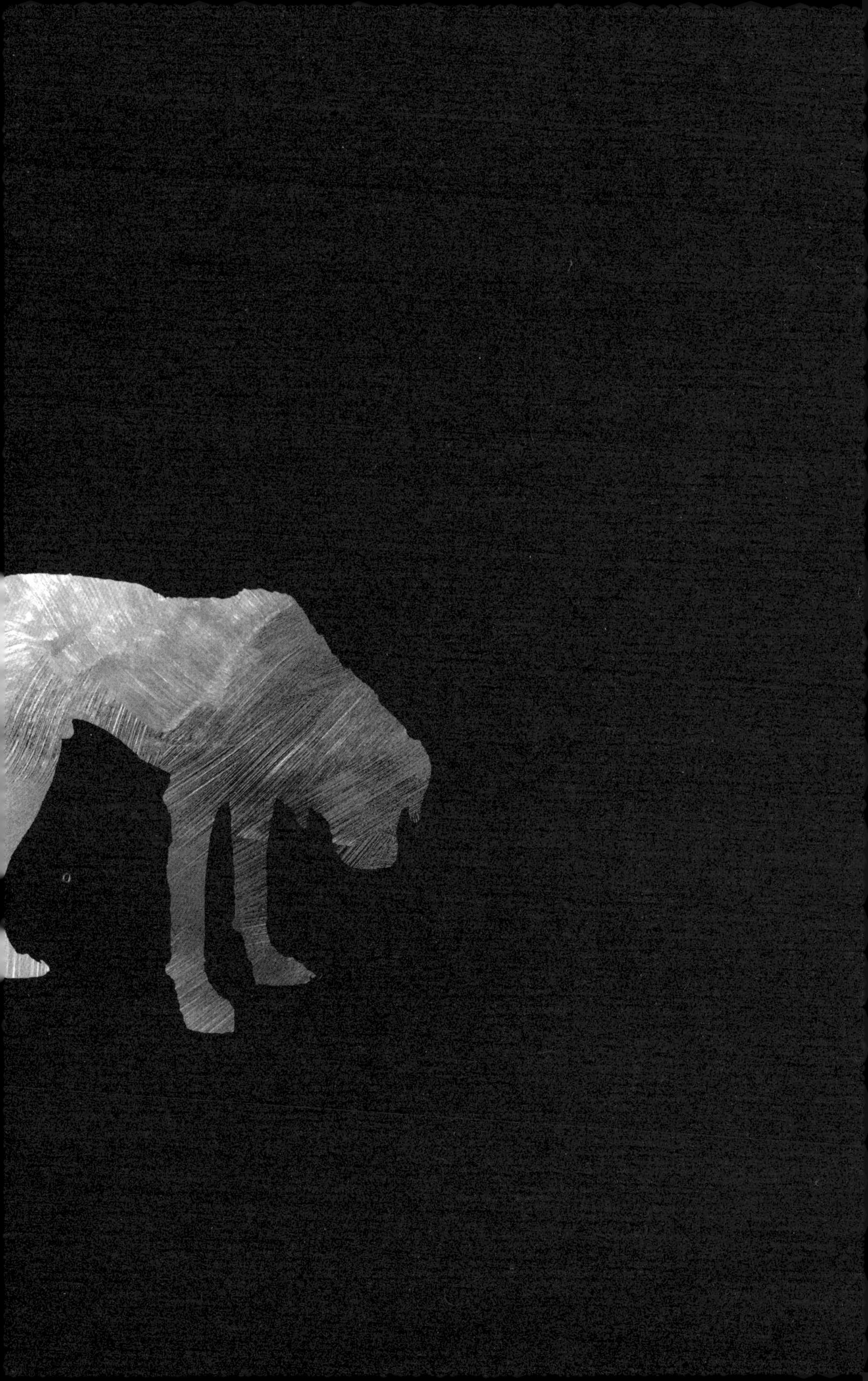

Samovar

When I walk down the road
The boys want me…
— Finnish folk song

First light temblor—
framed by the smeared train glass, dawn crowns
out of the mother goat of night
on her knees in Siberia, on cold ground,
the purple sac of morning
draining from her, the new day
wriggling beneath her,
it bleats, blind, wriggling on ice,
the mother's blood tongue
licking its face, it bleats, bleats, stumbles,
crawling out of birth steam
toward our Trans-Mongolian train,
the *Yingwoche*, fern green,
gliding heavy over the snow,
our house in the sky, our Zeppelin,
quiet as thunder, *east, east, east,*
six days Moscow to Beijing.
Tiina sings in Finnish, she peers out,
O my Baltic Medea, ferocious
and kind, all day we are vampires
hissing, talking gibberish,
bracing each other with laughter
and sex against the cruel
and absolute white nullity of Russia,
in our cozy cabin,
its pleasant reek of ramen,

affection, sweat. Siberian winds!
Forests spin by, birches:
spokes in a wheel
through which a light a light
persistent and dim
                                        flickers, forked,
a film projector stammering.
We roll, languid, deliberate, *east,*
east, uninvited callers, clumsy wedding guests,
thankless visitors, Eurotrash,
our rucksacks stuffed with vodka and
iPhones and suburban scorn.
When I was a graying Peter Pan
without home or girl,
Tiina hovered under me
in a hotel in Piraeus, blonde specter
in the dark, one finger
on my back: next morning,
waiting for a boat, we crouched
over a sparrow, wing shattered,
pushing itself in frenzied
circles, dogs closing in, and when
at last Tiina shut her eyes
I crushed it in my palm.
Our sixteen cars limp, *boo-huh,*
boo-huh, pulling out of Omsk,
its turquoise station,
its brokenhearted grain elevator,
its old women clearing snow
with sticks. Moon rising on the tall hats
of Krasnoyarsk, a frozen river,
the scroll unfolds, eternity,
still as ever as our spines tremble
and the Samovar
                                        drips, cylindrical genius,

corner of our car, in our dreams
a demiurge, Vishnu, many-fauceted,
our bride, our Jerusalem,
dust devil, enacting the goblin,
assuaging the lonely, *drips*,
hot and calm as thought itself,
drips. In the four directions we glide,
days are epochs, the tall birches
of Kirov reach for heaven
and give up part way. Our conductor,
Chinese, cool as they come,
gazes at a compact mirror,
combs his thin black hair,
our Master, reticent champion,
lord of every dust bunny in the car;
emissary of the Samovar,
he sips tea, shells seeds, scowls,
elbow-deep in pig viscera.
As I plod half-asleep
to the toilet, he transcribes
my dream into his log,
the one where I swim underwater
beside a fern-green snake
that swallows the white firmament
and coughs white coal.
When I was a young husband,
my wife ironed laundry
half-naked, I crouched in the bathroom,
watching her, pulling on
my ache, breathless,
choking,
               unable to cry. *Его послали*
считать берез в Сибирь! roars Dmitri,
hammered, hammering
the small table with his fist,

spraying a Dutch girl
with pickle juice. O beautiful Dutch girl
in your ice-blue dress, you
whose legs have never been broken
by your jealous brothers
or by anyone, do you feel
how lucky we are?
These Russian mothers
playing mahjong on suitcases,
laughing without shame,
they are the descendants of us all,
our dear children, and their kids
who have made a game
of jumping into each other's arms
our ancestors. The Samovar
grows prescient, filled with such
good will, we acolytes know
we'll find every bag
of lost luggage, we'll arrive
at Angarsk, at the snowy
roofs of Irkutsk, well on time.
Tiina, missing her cat,
sings, *Soft kitty, warm kitty,*
little ball of fur ... I lock
the door, slide my hand
inside her black dress,
pressing her flat on the narrow bed.
When I was a stripling,
spoiled, crucified
by megalomaniac shyness
and fantasies of June,
June walked with me in the rain,
her striped shirt wet,
small nipples hard,

we were new animals
licking each other's faces,
my childhood receding
like roadkill in a rearview mirror.
Happy kitty, sleepy kitty,
purr purr purr, shacks and fences
out the glass, beyond
attention, slosh in the brainpan,
like urine in a steel toilet
—and lumber, lumber
where gulags were. Tin loudspeakers
of Novosibirsk bleat and bleat
an ontology of discipline;
lumberjacks sucking on cigarettes,
a power pole their mute
witness, it kneels in snow,
its arm broken. It's a mistake
to think of the train
                                        on a single track,
or moving through time,
or moving at all, we are so still
it's unbearable and this fluid
urgency *boo-huh boo-huh* a trance
granting us a child's joy,
while this rocking this rocking to sleep
invites us into a reverie
too hot to touch,
a dream the Samovar is having,
we enter through a door
left ajar by our Master
into the coal furnace of self,
Minäpä sen olen se pikkuinen likka
ja olen kuin viulun kieli,
the train a snail shell curling in on itself,

trapped in amber,
an immense tremulous
pause. We reach out
into the blurred dark between cars,
our own hands appearing
behind us, grazing us
with memory. When I was a kid
in the forest of Bear River,
Steven and I were cosmonaut cowboys
in the last tent on earth,
I took his gun in my mouth
and there were foxes, we saw them
treading silent among
venomous orange mushrooms.
Where, we ask the Samovar,
will you lead us? Trans-Mongolia,
it answers. Is that, we ask,
a *place?*
            The rusted stairs of Tyumen!
The green fences of Ilanskaya!
Potato piroshki, five rubles!
Towns and towns of oil tanks
like coffee cups left in the snow.
Technology our simpleton,
boo-huh!, our Master its muscle,
Samovar-mind, cabin-eyes.
It is a mistake to think
the train exists in space
—it rolls *elsewhere*, tendering
a blur-line subterfuge
of snow, all we can grasp,
to our gullible senses.
The scroll unfolds, the Samovar drips,
and if you hear a baby skreighing

or a chicken behind a door,
or lovers in the toilet,
just ignore them,
the card players, the quarrelers,
as you would ignore
one of your own chaotic whims,
for everything you stole
has been returned
to its country of origin,
nations have been disbanded,
this life a shard of coal
offered to the open
fireplace
            of snow. When I was a baby,
wheeled by Jean my mother
in a supermarket maze,
I sat afloat in a shopping cart
of tangerines, a box
of Frosted Flakes my raft,
staring down the checkout girl,
my hard-on a lit match
poking out of my diaper.
O Samovar, I'm sure you had reason
to make me wait in my cabin
all these years, alone,
without brothers, sisters—
perhaps because I have broken
my vows to you
every day of my life?
I will try—I tell the Samovar,
smoking my Arthur Avenue cigar
between the cars—to write
in a language of snow,
and suck the icicles of death.

Tiina, eyes fluttering,
speaks out of her dream:
On a white field, she says,
the animals gather and are white.
A story of the train, her voice
that of the Samovar-
prophet, laboring for us,
we who do not thank it
or even notice it, we the separate,
scared, drained, clean,
too clean—so the Samovar
asks, with Tiina's lips,
How, ruiners, did you get
this clean?
                Great *Yingwoche*,
I lay my head on you
as on the breast of a giraffe,
your heart deep within you
white-hot, combusting. Ember sky,
my hunger is lethal. First stars,
I am a worm within
the ones I love. On the back
of Jean's bike, I held
the groceries, that was my job,
when we hit a pebble
we fell in the gravel
and I clutched that spilling bag
as if it were my soul.
I wake hugging my backpack,
Tiina absent. It snows
on the gray houses like nothingness
and beyond the wall
they are rolling bones,
I feel it, dusk throbs,

infinite cobalt blue,
serpentine, lightheaded
as a baby after a rage,
while a train thunders the other way
in arrant dark or a dog
dripping with blood
approaches the fire
or a psychopomp, mouth bleeding,
points to you and …
Tiina is not in the hall
but an old man—is it Tiina?—
stoops like a branch,
peeks from between cars
with cupped hands
through glass, as if scoping out
a good place to be born.

At the Củ Chi Tunnels

Soldiers, says our guide, are moles.
"Moles dig 250 feet a night.
In the Resistance War against America,
our Viet Cong crawled in dirt
with scorpions and dioxin. For liberty.
Liberty," he repeats, standing over
a tunnel. We lower ourselves into
that nightmare. I'm on a Hong Kong metro
crammed with commuters.
A young businessman holds his head
in his hands. On TV monitors,
a mob in Beijing protests Japan.
They, the Chinese, want the Diaoyu Islands.
They bear torches, like angels.
Smoke pours off them. In my dream,
a girl stands in a dioxin forest.
She speaks but I don't understand.
She climbs down a hole,
I follow. We are ants in a tunnel.
She presses her ant-face
on a glass wall. An army of ants
stops behind her. I see now
she is Joan of Arc. She points out
to a table of ant farms like our own,
and beyond that to a window,
nighttime, infinite sparkling dark:
tales of ancestors sketched
with the glittering eyes of colossal
dancing ants, spinning ants,
galactic ants in their tunnels.

A Girl on Khaosan Road Selling Lottery Tickets Gently Hides Her Two Withered Arms

and I crack, trembling with strangled frustration
under a waterfall of tourists.
Slow down, breathe. The scene clears.
A legless man with a tin cup
drags himself past. Sorrow demanding balance,
aching to be acknowledged.
Not reaching for my wallet
makes a land mine in my temple
shudder, click. Sleepwalker, wake.
Walk slower than backpackers,
hawkers, hippies, drunks. *Just so.*
Dread sinks from head to stomach to balls,
and overboard to sea bottom. Let it.
Lift the left foot, the right plays along.
Can I walk so slow?
Beside a big TV, a scrawny cat,
utterly still. A Theravāda monk, snail
in a forest, out-slows me,
which is comforting. I, disheveled
hummingbird, absurd. A fire in my shoulders
and stomach begs me: holler, leap,
anything. It feels so good to resist, to stop,
despite this truck at my chest,
overloaded with bags of tamarind, honking bitterly.

Public Cremation, Pashupatinath Temple, Kathmandu

No promise of gray in your hair, now basted
with damp hay. Your face fleshy, healthy.
You were young, rich. Hard to tell if you were good.
Nobody is crying. Where is your mother?
They, your cousins and uncles, dip your smooth
feet in the gray bilge smog-trickle of Bagmati River.
A crowd leans toward the spectacle
on a bridge that doves sail under. Upriver,
a woman washes her feet vigorously.
They wrap your dark penis in cloth. Each
touches your hair. All part of the ceremony.
Nobody blinks when a tourist cuts in
to take a selfie with you. Monkeys slide down
a temple roof. Boys hock a loogie
over the ghat. Nepali pop on a shrill radio.
They find a note in your pocket and look it over.
They lay a torch at your throat. Ashes
and butterflies issue forth. Sadhus—
the dead ones, cohorts of ghosts,
stoned gods, thinking as stones think
—walk about as if lost. Your thighs
ash, your robe butterflies. Your toes boil.
That which was dark and alchemical
turns to flies, butterflies. Your thick hair smoke
and your eyes butterflies. Your foot
is yellow and your thigh bone sticks out.
Hand open, palm charred. Your ribs revealed.
When two monkeys hump in the ford,
the crowd laughs loudly and without malice.

Naked Woman at a Roadside Buffet

On the riverbank, she pours sand
onto her long black hair,
diva at a mirror. She holds the air, gently,
as if breastfeeding the clouds.
She lashes out at jeans, yanking them
up her left leg. Boys point, laugh.
She drops the jeans, threads
the lunch tables where we eat *dal bhat*,
her eyes dark, wide,
glowering, pubic hair black,
bursting, legs sinewy, breasts flat.
Shame ripples across us.
We tuck away our phones.
We cover children's eyes.
We board the bus. Our driver,
chewing his thick moustache, backs out,
one eye glued to the naked woman
standing in dust, a revenant.
We all watch her. She spasms, writhing,
her mouth forming non-words,
swallowing lightning, some river
flooding and my reasons
for being cruel are false, all false.
Our tires spin in the dirt.

One Given When I'd Ceased to Look

Tiina vomits dry mustard,
wipes her mouth,
wary of me, ferocious.
I take a walk.
On the night street,
dust, insecticide, glass malls.
When power cuts out,
it's a village, dark and quiet, briefly.
Solar generators kicking in
sound like crashing helicopters.
A single light bulb in a shop
surges, blinks,
revealing arches, gates, chicken claws
on a blood string. Behold
the great design: Kathmandu!
At the threshold of the visible,
candles flicker. A sandstone monarch grins.
At a Eucharistic garbage fire,
a skeletal white dog
steps out and follows me
along the street. She hobbles,
so I match her pace. She pauses
when I pause, looking up.
I offer bread, she isn't hungry.
At a clamorous intersection
I kneel, holding her thin head
in my hands, birds
darting past in the oily dark.
Looking into my eyes,
she slackens, leaning
her injured leg on my arm.

Dying in Dharamsala

Carlos grew skinny in those months.
So very light
on the back of my Enfield,
a kind of human bird.
Dogs on the dirt roads
licked their sores as we drove by.
I sit with friends
on the rugs of his room,
listening to him talk
for hours, him on his bed
amid dharma texts
and a photo of Amma,
his beloved hugging guru.
He is excited, waving an arm,
more an insect claw
than the brawny lifeguard arm
he used to have.
Vague sounds reach us
from the road: bulls lowing,
kids chattering in Hindi.
Carlos, on his right side,
resembles Reclining Buddha
except that he is detailing
his bowel movements,
each herb and powder
he's ingested,
to invite us into a realm
where he is not sick,
where he has cured himself
with tinctures.
And we believe it,

how could we not believe it?
For God's sake,
just look at his elfin grin,
his angel-fierce
mischievous eyes.
He is beautiful. And yet
something wobbles,
out of true, some top spinning
in the shadow of his words
that might fall
if he stops talking.

By the Halal Chicken Shop

As I'm driving,
Tiina hops off the Enfield
in traffic, trots into an alley
after a hurt puppy.
I find her in a doorless
burnt-out room.
Three or four small boys
smiling. One of them tilts up
a charred bed: under it,
puppies gnaw the body
of a dead brethren, as if nursing.
I hand the hurt one
to Tiina. It is all ribs.
Shit smeared
on muzzle and eye.
Grandma, do you remember Tiina?
You met her once
just before you were gone.
She is not Catholic
but you might like her
anyway. Is she good enough,
you ask, for my John Wall?
Just look how she holds
the filthy puppy
against her turquoise coat
in front of the halal shop.

Parking Lot, Tibetan Parliament-in-Exile, Noon

A Tibetan woman in a striped apron
feeds a donkey
watermelon slices.
Other donkeys
bearing great sacks of bricks
wait their turn.
They are modest,
patient. Not ravenous.
It is not essential to know
that this woman
(she who now pets
the straw mane of the donkey,
making his brown eyes
go sleepy and soft)
had a son named Chaku
who at fifteen
soaked himself in petrol,
lit a match and held it
base of his throat
as if it were the first noble truth,
and that it was she
who found him,
she who wrapped
the black feathers of his body
in a blanket.
Today it is hot.
The sun a butter lamp.

One monkey sits
in a tree. One hawk circles.
We walk slow
impossibly slow
past the shadowless donkey
that chews the sweet
flesh of the watermelon
with mild surprise.

A Stop on the Night Bus

Under the garbage I'm pissing on
water mutters, a river.
A field of sugar cane swells
to a sexual bursting.
Predawn calls to prayer.
What an odd feeling,
as if *inside* night itself.
Night my exoskeleton.
A boy flips an omelet over a fire
exaggeratedly, a dance
of elbows. A narrow
red dog edges the light.
The boy threatens him
with a spatula. The dog limps—
it is horrible to watch
—past a lady munching on
an omelet. (Once past
he flashes into the dark
sans limp!) Gestation
used to mean carried by a craft
as in a boat or a mother.
When I was a baby
Dr. Levin told my mother
I was pigeon-toed:
left foot "eccentric." For months
my mother massaged
my soft bones.
When our mothers are dead
and we find ourselves
askew, what massages us?

Out of trash bag tents
come the ditchdiggers.
Beside the road
the first pickaxes
(the way certain mere words
placed together
resemble truth itself)
are glittering.

Cryptoscopophilia

At the Bhagsu Waterfall,
girls wade in
wrapped in saris.
Mothers wave from tables,
babies on laps.
Boys and men, louder,
shout, dive, splash
in their underwear
at the deep end of the cold
snowmelt. I think
I am smiling.
Behind me
in the dark of cut stone
a Punjabi kid
in his first beard
holds his elbow
from which a needle
is withdrawn
by a fat man,
sweating, smirking at me,
head bobbing, to say
It is *our* business,
look away tourist.
Now the boy teeters
at water's edge,
his light dim, fluttering.
I stare at him,
I can't help it,
through the mist window.
The goblins,
spotting me,
scramble out
in every direction.

Delirious in the Pink House

I am the big flabby American poet,
the one in the over-
sized Pink House
in a village in the Himalayas.
That's me on the roof
in my green kurta
dancing in the afternoon!
I stand stalwart on the terrace
as if it were the crow's nest
of a ship. I peek out
the barred windows,
villain in a Russian silent film.
After writing a poem
I stand up with great pleasure,
I howl my happiness!
Local men beside a brushfire
stop their conversation,
staring. Old women glower,
stooped over their brooms.
Families walking by
give the Pink House
a wide berth. What do I care?
I run out into the road
high-fiving paupers,
tousling the hair of children.
They draw away slightly
but my poetry is a magic wand:
I call out, *you* (cow)
rhyme with *that* (plow)!
That (kite) is a metaphor
for *you* (little girl)!
Speak to me, O goatherd,
of the simple life!

Teach me suffering!
Take me on the goat trails
of the heart! O villagers,
help me praise the goat
and the goatless goat!
(I write all this down.
It is all gold.) There is a funeral
in progress by the river.
A mother weeps
beside her burning son.
I dance around them
twirling. How can I help it?
They are so pretty
in their bright purple outfits.
I want, I tell the living
and the dead, to be free,
free as this woman,
eyes gray as the pan of gravel
she carries on her head,
under these picturesque hills!
And when the trash in the streams
and the babies in rags
sadden me, I just climb aboard
the Pink House
as it drifts on the dusk
toward sleep.

Beauty Too Close

Almost asleep, heartbeat
echoing in my skull,
there comes a silence
with a roaring in it.
I stumble outside.
There is our tomcat, yowling,
a rat in his mouth.
I pour water on him.
He steps away
with the rat. I lean in,
near as I can. The rat
blinks, hanging there,
slack, gory, walleyed,
front teeth long and yellow,
a grizzled banjo player
who smoked himself hoarse
years ago. Our cat
leaves the body
by the door. I lie in bed
picturing that face,
its weird glow,
remembering that one year
I grew thin:
turning to paper
and then ash.
How could I forget
that beauty will destroy us?
I hear wings
and
the rat is gone.

Dead Calf by the Road

on gravel, guts sliding out
of the bowl of itself
like oatmeal, tailbone
a white hammer
obtruding the soft
kidskin, head tucked in
as if napping. I pull
the heavy Enfield
off the road.
Crows on the back
of the calf flap off.
Out of the church
in the hollow behind my right eye,
I see the crows
on their branches,
heads cocked, itching to feast.
It is worse because
the calf did not carry
a gun to school
or insult her friends
but just walked very gently
beside her mother.
They didn't tell her
they don't tell you
about dying on a road,
crows the only flags upon you
in a hornetsong wind.

Sipping Tequila with a Friend on My Roof under the Cold Blowtorch Moon

A whirlwind of joy rumbles
utterly quiet
just above my head
while the puppies,
the mangy feral puppies
on the stairs
behind our house,
shiver in the cold.
What does it say about me
that I can feel joy
while bad things
happen? Is joy a thief
climbing in the window
we should clobber
over the head?
As Achilles and Briseis
in their war tent
pour goatskins of wine
on each other's faces,
Hector drags Patroclus
over the rocks.
Even as I lean over this poem,
my friend is being
torn to rags by AIDS.
Each morning
I lie in the grass
in feverish sunlight
as the mud-slathered puppies,
little horses, gallop
all over me and trot off

delighted
to forage the river of garbage
for food. It is forbidden
to love hurt things
more than nature does.
But joy, joy is the taproot.
We are allowed
to feel it. From my roof
I hear them, yipping.
That satyric chorus.
The bliss born of agony.

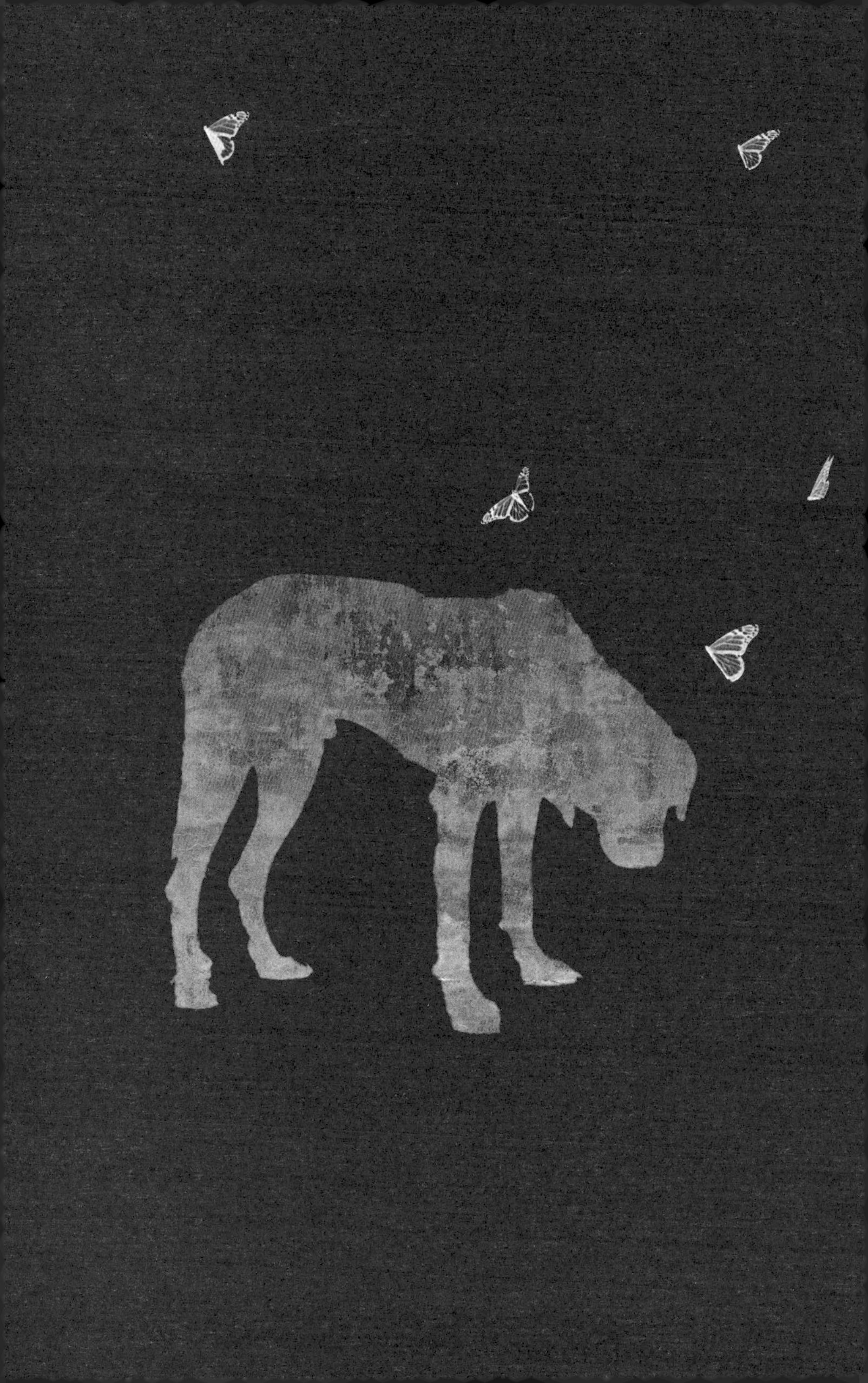

Dukkha

The water is moving
The road gushes
Like an autistic child the road collapses
We *hear* it
Ears against the mist
An unembellished grayness
A waterfall a river

What drifts through these barred windows
I lean into a book
A river overruns its banks
Plastic blossoms
Butterflies born of plastic
Dappled things
Listen it is the shopkeeper
Slapping the monsoon road
With a white rag!

Tiina sleeps at home
She has a low fever
All afternoon she sleeps
I text her from my writing room
More a cell really
Tin ceiling hard bed
I am wrapped in blankets
A worried pupa

My book is Tagore's translation of Kabīr
Windows barred against
The water moving
With all its heart the rain-bird

longs for the shower of rain;
But upon whose love does the Lover
concentrate His entire life?

I am frazzled yes
Trying in these weeks to write
About Hong Kong
Where Tiina and I lived
Tai Po a suburb
We threw parties drank wine
Ordered groceries online
Against a backdrop of humans
Infinite tenements
Those rotting logs they live beneath
We had to get out
To erase the flawed portrait
We were painting
Of ourselves

Monsoon season in Dharamsala
The sun obscured
The mold grandiloquent
The spores!
Blooming in lungs
In the mountains like snow
Virulent mud
We surrender to water
To the ubiquitous Lay's chip bags
Among prayer flags
On the steep green cliffs
Here is a white donkey on a chain
Here is an old man
Washing his beard
In rainwater gushing off a roof

Beside the road
Men burn the leavings and debris
Fires punctuate the way
Putrefied lychee zucchini rinds
Finches' wings
Carbon monoxide beedi cigarettes
Smoldering
Men in circles palms bright
Surrendering
Did you know humans
Can detect a drop of musk in a concert hall?
Did you know a bride
Is burned every hour in Bharat?

Kabīr the mystic the saint
Gurus blossom out of him and sects
Sant Mat is one of those
Radhasoamis
The portrait my parents have painted
Since the 1970s
Of themselves

A rickshaw in a great hurry
Honks
Splashes a girl in a green sari
Her reply a nice flamenco stomp
Right foot in a puddle
A palmreader squats on bricks
A corn seller fans a flame
The firecoal horns of Shiva
Simmering

I lay on my back
I have been wondering

What pain we share
And where we intersect
My tin ceiling drips
The hand of mist reaching in
I'm anxious about Tiina
Almost time to bring her dinner
It cannot be told
by the words of the mouth
Kabīr you come like tears
After a long joy

Four Punjabis on a purple Enfield
Festooned with flags
They writhe and kick and sing!
Easy to say they are fools
But it might well be
Something else

My room a brick hut
On the roof of a family home
Gaddis
Once nomadic shepherds
Now shop owners
The husband sells crystals
To Israeli travelers
The wife in her flowering sari
Shakes a heavy blanket
Light maroon
Lotuses
Screams at her children

Honk your horns O Delhi tourists
Annihilate birdsong
Did you know to a sparrow

The human voice is low rumbling
Distant thunder?
Dogs and donkeys
Make a house of your dust

My neighbor is Dorje
He knocks each afternoon
Hungry to speak
Of his homeland Tibet
His eyes stripped of all disguises
But misfortune

To escape Tibet
Dorje walked across Nepal
A mountain range
This was fifteen years ago
He was a teenager
American filmmakers
Made a documentary about him

Speaking to him I can smell
My ignorance
My skin emits a whiff
A kind of burning putrefaction
I tire of smelling it
A man howls Hindi songs
On the hill above

Dorje hands me a glass
A thick hot glass
Good tea from China he says
Leaves drowning at the top
Like insects
Animals clambering in rubble

He hears Tibet news
On WeChat
Last night the Chinese he says
Arrested a Tibetan leader
For no reason
Hundreds protested
Police fired into the crowd
Men and women fell
A man hanged himself in jail
His body hovering
All night above the others

I read Dorje from Kabīr
If you have not drunk of the nectar of that One Love,
what boots it though you
should purge yourself of all stains?
Dorje stares at me

A cross-eyed man on the road
Bright hula hoops
On each arm
Limps
Out of another world

The second noble truth
Dorje explains
As Gaddi children
Run to and fro
Shouting tossing firecrackers
Is the sadness of *trying* to hold
What is changing
As if there were something
Some essence

To be held
This misunderstanding
Causes suffering
Dukkha

I am not Buddhist I say
Grinning and Dorje
Just stares
Sips his tea
Gaddi children toss candy wrappers
Into a tree

The Gaddi daughter
Has hard eyes
I have seen her haul bricks
As her brother plays
With a cricket bat
Today she scrubs metal dishes
Beside a goat
Her brother rides his bicycle
Around her in circles
Singing
Ringing his bell

I text Tiina
O servant, where dost thou seek Me?
Lo! I am beside thee
She writes back
LOL

In an expat café I sip chai
The room shakes
An earthquake resembling a god

Heaves us
We run out of the room
Spilling our drinks
As if no pain has ever been felt
By anyone

In 1905 an earthquake wiped this village clear

Farm animals walk free
Goats sheep horses
Tiptoe the roads
A scooter lets rip a banshee wail
A cow turns her head
Shyly

I hear a hawk screech
I open my door
It is a kitten mewling
How delicious
To mistake a sound
The kitten feral
Hungry
Cold eyes staring

A dog with a crushed back leg
Limps among cars
Like an earthquake
But silent
Such beauty on this road
Where the Tibetan nun was raped

I am moved by fancies that are curled
Around these animals
What drifts in our windows

Through the bars
What we would change violently
What we hold on the skin

I walk the mud road
Whispering my Hindi homework
I stop to watch a girl *(larakī)*
Pat a dog *(kuttā)*
It is common to hear a girl called *kutiyā*
"Bitch"

Larakī kuttā kutiyā larakī kuttā kutiyā

A line of Kabīr clings
O bodiless one!
do not sit on your doorstep; go forth and bathe yourself
in that rain
I will I will I will

Astonishment our bread
The road floods its banks
The blood that pulls us
Into its current
Does not stop at the edges
Of the body
Flows into the world
Urges us
Along the chaotic muddy path
Prods like a goat
With a twisted horn

Who are they that walk the road?
Beloved ones
They had nothing

Yet I was jealous
I wanted what they had

Bring your face nearer to His ear
A grumbling sound
Thunder
I am not anything

Over the hill two Gaddi men
Carry a long metal sheet
Not thunder
But how good it feels
To misunderstand

On a North Train to Casarsa, Midwinter, Thinking of *Franny and Zooey*

A man has thrown himself on the tracks,
we stop three hours in Cesena. *Polizia, Ambulanza*—
we crane to look from the platform.
The station typical, nice. Coffee bar,
teen girls on mobile phones. A circle of *signori*
smoking, as in the old days. Beyond,
a hard night to die: gray, moonless. Far-off,
yellow streetlights divide earth from sky.
An Albanian vendor sells candy and newspapers
that say, *"Romanziere J.D. Salinger Morto."*
Salinger, gone. Zooey, my favorite character
of all time, flashes before me. Ferocious Zooey.
Waving his cigar, berating Franny, his sister,
for refusing their mother's consecrated soup.
For twenty years I have imitated Zooey shaving,
staring into his own eyes: "neutral territory,
a no man's land in a private war against narcissism."
We arrive at Casarsa late. I light a Toscano
cigar. Cypresses line the cemetery road. I hop
the wall. On each gravestone, an oval photo
of the dead. Tiny lightbulbs a fusillade in fog,
a glittering underwater realm. A dog barks.
At last I find him: Pasolini. Two white marble
grave markers, the poet and his mother Susanna.
I tell them how far I've come for this honor.
"Che bello conoscervi," I say, and curl up
in the gravel under a tree beside them.

Bergamo Airport, 3:30 a.m.

We wake and when we wake we are awful.
I did not notice in daylight. Even the lovely Arab family,
sleeping with hands in each other's hair,
a hydra of love—even the two Scandinavian girls
turning in their sleeping bags, Viking pupas—
lack entirely in innocence. I see it in this boy's soft-
tough face: tucked under his mother's arm, with his gadgetry
and lavish parka, frowning like a pitiless banker.
He wants what he wants. He hates what he has.
He craves what he has not got. You can smell it on him.
I try to like him but can't. He sings the songs of children
and laughs a child's laugh, but he is not a child. Blood
of the twentieth century on his fingers. Stalin, Nixon.
You can see it in his eyes, boredom. No, exhaustion.
Barbwired in by freedom itself: a longing for the grave.
Seeing no other choice, he stands. He joins the line
beside his baby sister. Ungrateful.

Bullfight, Plaza México

The beardless matador
in his suit of lights
whirls on the dust, O teen god
jabbing jabbing
the mortal bull
with long feathered blades
simply, without force,
like tearing a web,
as if he made his own fate
like the spheres.
The bull snorts
a proud distress call.
Clamor brawls
along the stands. A father
of three gleeful boys
in Yankees hats
squirts mescal into my mouth
from his canteen
and the fifth bull thrashes
sideways out the gate
into the light,
moth with a torn wing
crouching
immutable
long horns of a gothic church
and in my delirium
I call for you, Ruka,
my skinny sickly
dog, I think the bull
they're butchering
is you. Picadors

pierce your paws,
roll you onto a sled,
horses drag you
out of the circle,
out of the light,
your great head lolling
on sand. This godless earth,
grainy photocopy
of heaven.
We cannot close our eyes
against the parade
of bodies rolling past.
We eat our peanuts,
we sip our Cokes,
we call out, *Mas! Mas!*
Starving for the dark.
Give us *more*,
we call, *more* of the dark,
like oracles.

The human sat up in bed, rubbed his eyes. The window and door were *wrong*. The mountains outside, wrong. It all seemed out of sync, as if the gods that rearrange the world at night had put it back wrong. He shut his eyes, whispered to himself, "*C'mon,* li'l cutiepie." Felt nothing. His heart an arctic moon in infinite space.

He stepped out for a walk, passing the farm with the hairy black goats, whose collective bleating make a woozy circus music. Whose throats will be cut at the end of the month. The farmer, whose soil is desiccated, whose son's ribs stick out, waved. He waved back, rubbed his eyes, peered up at the mountains.

Was there nothing good on earth? He stopped under a pine tree struck by lightning, needles at his feet. That's how he felt! He whispered, softly, to himself, "Little cutiepie, little sailorboy, little pulsebeat," and smiled despite himself. *"You,"* he whispered, slowing to hear it, "are the humble boatman who helps travelers over stormy waters." He snorted, shook his head like a bride. How absurd: he was neither humble nor a boatman. But he felt better. Nothing had changed, he knew. Still the neighbor's dog had lesions around its eyes resembling holes in the ice. Still the mountains, overmined for shale, were collapsing. Nevertheless, some hidden chamber within him had swung open. Now he felt the plenty of it.

There, before him, his own wife in the doorway of their home. A butterfly cut a jagged line in the air around her. And green parrots, above, crossing the valley like a whirling tree.

NOTES

Epigraph: The French New Wave film *Hiroshima Mon Amour* (1959) was directed by Alain Resnais and written by Marguerite Duras (book by Grove Press, 1961). Translated from the French by Richard Seaver.

Smog Mother:

In June 2014, a military coup took place in Bangkok. The anti-democratic Thai army, under the name The National Council for Peace and Order (NCPO), declared martial law, deploying troops and taking control of the country. They suspended the constitution and imposed a curfew. Thai citizens marched in the streets, foreign nationals evacuated by the thousands, and some—such as Sutin Tharatin, a pro-democracy protester shot while giving a speech in the back of a truck—were assassinated. The NCPO remained in power for five years, until 2019.

The Louise Glück passage comes at the end of "Child Crying Out," in *Ararat* (1990).

The Siriraj Medical Museum, or "Museum of Death," is full of "medical oddities" preserved in jars with formaldehyde, such as conjoined twins, "pickled punks," and diseased bodily organs. The most famous exhibit, mummified serial killer Si Quey, was finally cremated in 2020 after sixty years on public display.

The lines "When your heart marches out to die / When you march out to kill" are borrowed from César Vallejo's long poem, "Hymn to the Volunteers for the Republic" ("Himno a Los Voluntarios de la República"), in *Spain, Take this Cup from Me* (*España, Aparta de mí este Cáliz*, 1939; Grove Press translation, 1974), in which Vallejo applies a humanist lens to the Spanish Civil War. My poem, its rhythms and sympathies, owes a debt to Vallejo's book.

The line from Lao Tzu is from chapter 47 of the *Tao Te Ching.*

Khruba Siwichai (1878-1939) was a Thai Buddhist monk (Theravāda lineage), best known for building temples, political conflict with local authorities, and personal charisma.

King Bhumibol Adulyadej (1927-2016), the highly respected ninth monarch of Thailand, reigned for over seventy years, making him the second-longest reigning monarch of all time. During his life, and after as well, he was protected by some of the strictest *lèse-majesté* laws in the world, meaning it was illegal to defame, insult or threaten him, with a threat of imprisonment for three to fifteen years. The king acknowledged the 2014 coup, but did not initially approve of it. Later, he formally appointed the anti-democracy leader General Prayut Chan-o-cha to run the country, giving his royal endorsement.

Martin Luther used the expression "sin bravely" ("*pecca fortiter*") in a letter to Philip Melanchthon on August 1, 1521.

The Yeats lines come from "A General Introduction for my Work" (written in 1937 for a collected edition that was never published).

Samovar:

The Trans-Mongolian rail trip is 4,735 miles, eight days, six time zones, Moscow to Beijing. The rail cars are coal-heated. At one end of each car is a toilet, and at the other is a samovar: a giant, impressive hot-water kettle. The samovar, constantly spitting and humming, provides an endless supply of hot water for tea, instant coffee, noodles, soups.

The epigraph is from Finnish folk-rock group Värttinä's 1991 song *"Miinan Laulu,"* inspired by a traditional folk melody. The lyrics describe a girl named Miina sizing up her wooers: "Oh, if I'd get that rose / stomped into the ground. / Oh, if I'd get that pretty boy / lured to my side." Here's the full stanza the epigraph is taken from: "I'm a small girl / Like a violin string / When I walk down the road / The boys want me." (In Finnish: *"Minäpä sen olen se pikkuinen likka / ja olen kuin viulun kieli. / Kun minä maantietä kävelen, / niin poikien tekkee mieli."*) The first two of those Finnish lines occur later in "Samovar." (Nb. Google Translate renders "I'm a small girl / Like a violin string" as "Let me be that little bastard / And I am like the tongue of a violin.")

"*Его послали считать берез в Сибирь*" is a Russian proverb: "He has been sent to count the birches in Siberia." Presumably, an interminable punishment.

"Soft Kitty" is an old children's song. The tune originates from nineteenth century Poland, a lullaby called "*Wlazł kotek na płotek*" written by Oskar Kolberg and composed by Stanisław Moniuszko. I learned it from the TV show *The Big Bang Theory*.

Dying in Dharamsala:

Dharamsala, nestled in the Indian Himalayas, is home to the 14th Dalai Lama and—since the Chinese occupation of Tibet in the early 1950s—is the present-day epicenter of Tibetan Buddhism.

Mātā Amritānandamayī Devī (born 1953), known as Amma ("Mother"), is an Indian Hindu spiritual leader, revered as "the hugging saint." She has hugged more than 33 million people throughout the world over the last 30 years.

Parking Lot, Tibetan Parliament-in-Exile, Noon:

Since 2009, 157 Tibetans—many of them Buddhist monks—have burned themselves alive in Tibet, China, and India, to protest Chinese occupation of Tibet. There is a debate in the Tibetan community as to whether those who self-immolate are heroes. The Dalai Lama, a respected voice of peace and reason, remains neutral, but does not seem to support it.

The Four Noble Truths are fundamental to Buddhist teaching: 1. Life is suffering (Suffering); 2. The cause of suffering is craving and fundamental ignorance (Origin); 3. Suffering can end because our awakened mind is always available to us (Cessation); 4. We can wake up if we follow the path (The Path).

Cryptoscopophilia:

This word is easy to find in pseudo-dictionaries online, such as urbandictionary.com, which defines it as "The urge to look through the windows of homes upon walking past them. Usually done for sexual satisfaction/curiousity [sic] reasons." The OED, which doesn't contain the whole word, defines the prefix *crypto-* as "concealed, not visible, not apparent" and *scopophilia* as "Sexual stimulation or satisfaction derived principally from looking; voyeurism."

Dukkha:

The Pali word *Dukkha* (Sanskrit *Dukhka*) describes a variety of unpleasant human experiences: "Suffering or discomfort which arises as a result of the transitory nature of all phenomena, and is inherent in every aspect of human existence; physical or mental affliction or disharmony" (OED). It's an important concept in Hinduism and Buddhism, commonly translated as suffering, unhappiness, pain or, generally, the fundamental unsatisfactoriness and painfulness of mundane life. *Dukkha* is strongly linked to the Four Noble Truths, especially the first.

The five italicized quotes (not including "*Larakī kuttā kutiyā …*") are by Kabīr, a 15th-century Indian mystic poet and saint, from *Songs of Kabir*, a 1915 book consisting of 100 poems translated into English by Rabindranath Tagore.

Bharat—derived from Sanskrit, *Bhārata Ganarājya*—is another name for the Indian subcontinent and the Republic of India.

On a North Train to Casarsa, Midwinter, Thinking of Franny and Zooey:

The quote is from J.D. Salinger's third book, *Franny and Zooey* (Little, Brown, 1961).

Pier Paolo Pasolini (1922-75) was an Italian film director, poet and intellectual. He was murdered in Rome and buried in his hometown, Casarsa, in the northern region of Friuli-Venezia Giulia.

Acknowledgments

My thanks to the editors of publications in which the following poems first appeared:

Alfred Gustav Press: *Dying in Dharamsala* (chapbook): "Dying in Dharamsala," "By the Halal Chicken Shop," "Parking Lot, Tibetan Parliament-in-Exile, Noon," "A Stop on the Night Bus," "Cryptoscopophilia," "Beauty Too Close," "Dead Calf by the Road," "Sipping Tequila with a Friend on My Roof under the Cold Blowtorch Moon"
Antigonish Review: "Bergamo Airport, 3:30 a.m."
Asia Literary Review: "Public Cremation, Pashupatinath Temple, Kathmandu"
Baseline Press: *Samovar/Dukkha* (chapbook)
Cortland Review: "An Old Man in Black Slippers at Rush Hour"
Fiddlehead: "Dithyramb for a Troubled Man in Yau Ma Tei," "100 Doves Released for Wedding Pictures at Swan Lake in Hefei, Anhui Province, China," and "Bathroom Attendant in Tai Po Megamall"
Freefall: "Naked Woman at a Roadside Buffet"
Grain: "A Girl on Khaosan Road Selling Lottery Tickets Gently Hides Her Two Withered Arms" and "One Given When I'd Ceased to Look"
Lake Effect: "At the Củ Chi Tunnels"
Literary Matters: "The human sat up in bed..."
Literary Review of Canada: "Delirious in the Pink House"
Looking Back at Hong Kong (Anthology, Cart Noodles Press): "Ode to Festival Walk Mall"
Malahat Review: "Smog Mother," "On a "North Train to Casarsa, Midwinter, Thinking of *Franny and Zooey*," and "Bullfight, Plaza México"
The Stinging Fly: "Fireflies"
Subtropics: "On a Metro at the Edge of Jungles where Tigers Walked"
Vallum: "Woman on a Hong Kong Bus at Night"

Thank you to Sun Man Ho, Blair Reeve, Matthew Wong, Akin Jeje, Kate Rogers, Collier Nogues, Peter Kennedy, Shawn Moseley, Laura Cook, Michael O'Sullivan, Ernie Hilbert, Luke Stromberg, Vasiliki Katsarou, Cameron MacKenzie, Tim Fitts, Steven Kleinman, Anthony Rivel, Kyle Brown-Watson, Indran Amirthanayagam, Fayyaz Vellani, Warren C. Longmire, Luke Bartolomeo, Ben Gallagher, Stephanie Bolster, Micheline Maylor, Brian Bartlett, Tonja Gunvaldsen Klaassen, Jami Macarty, James Arthur, and Ryan Wilson.

To Karen Schindler at Baseline Press for publishing the two long poems, "Samovar" and "*Dukkha*," as a single chapbook, *Samovar/Dukkha,* in 2016.

To the judges of the 2017 *Malahat Review* Long Poem Prize for choosing the title poem, "Smog Mother," as co-winner.

To David Zieroth at Alfred Gustav Press for publishing the poems in the fifth section (except "Delirious in the Pink House") as a chapbook called *Dying in Dharamsala* in 2018.

To Philadelphia Poet Laureate Trapeta B. Mayson for featuring "The human sat up in bed…" (on May 10, 2021, as "The Joy of Li'l Cutiepie") in Healing Verse Philly, a toll-free phone line that offered callers a 90-second poem by a Philadelphia poet.

To the Canada Council for the Arts for assistance during crucial stages in the development of this book.

To Jim Johnstone, brilliant editor, for letting me lean on him again.

To Palimpsest Press, especially Aimée Parent Dunn, for making me feel like part of the family.

To my parents, John and Jean, for raising me to think that if I had travel and art and people with good hearts in my life, the rest would fall into place.

To Tiina, for picking up every wounded animal she comes across, including me.

John Wall Barger is the author of five collections of poetry. His poems and critical writing have appeared in *American Poetry Review*, *Kenyon Review Online*, *ZYZZYVA*, *The Cincinnati Review*, *Poetry Ireland Review*, and *Best of the Best Canadian Poetry*. He's a contract editor with Frontenac House, and teaches in the BFA Program for Creative Writing at The University of the Arts in Philadelphia.